# CELEBRATING THE CHINESE NEW YEAR

## BY BARBARA M. LINDE

Gareth Stevens
PUBLISHING

Please visit our website, www.garethstevens.com. For a free color catalog of all our high-quality books, call toll free 1-800-542-2595 or fax 1-877-542-2596.

**Cataloging-in-Publication Data**

Names: Linde, Barbara M.
Title: Celebrating the Chinese New Year / Barbara M. Linde.
Description: New York : Gareth Stevens Publishing, 2020. | Series: The history of our holidays | Includes glossary and index.
Identifiers: ISBN 9781538238622 (pbk.) | ISBN 9781538238646 (library bound) | ISBN 9781538238639 (6 pack)
Subjects: LCSH: Chinese New Year–Juvenile literature. | Chinese New Year–History–Juvenile literature.
Classification: LCC GT4905.L57 2020 | DDC 394.261–dc23

Published in 2020 by
**Gareth Stevens Publishing**
111 East 14th Street, Suite 349
New York, NY 10003

Designer: Laura Bowen
Editor: Barbara M. Linde

Photo credits: Cover, p. 1 Pacific Press/LightRocket/Getty Images; pp. 2–24 (background texture) secondcorner/Shutterstock.com; pp. 3–24 (background flags) saicle/Shutterstock.com; p. 5 Photo Spirit/Shutterstock.com; p. 7 KPG_Payless/Shutterstock.com; p. 9 Tom Wang/Shutterstock.com; p. 11 mandritoiu/Shutterstock.com; p. 13 KK Tan/Shutterstock.com; p. 15 wong yu liang/Shutterstock.com; p. 17 Boontoom Sae-Kor/Shutterstock.com; p. 19 (top) Saigoneer/Shutterstock.com; p. 19 (bottom) Kit Leong/Shutterstock.com; p. 21 testing/Shutterstock.com.

CPSIA compliance information: Batch #CS19GS: For further information contact Gareth Stevens, New York, New York at 1-800-542-2595

# CONTENTS

A Cheerful Holiday . . . . . . . . . . . . . . 4

Different Dates. . . . . . . . . . . . . . . . . 6

How the Holiday Started . . . . . . . . . 8

Celebrating Around the World. . . . . 10

Goodbye, Bad Luck . . . . . . . . . . . . 12

Family Time . . . . . . . . . . . . . . . . 14

Lion and Dragon Dances. . . . . . . . 18

The Lantern Festival . . . . . . . . . . . 20

Glossary. . . . . . . . . . . . . . . . . . 22

For More Information. . . . . . . . . . 23

Index . . . . . . . . . . . . . . . . . . . 24

**Boldface** words appear in the glossary.

# A Cheerful Holiday

Fireworks light up the night sky. Loud firecrackers pop. Colorful lions, long dragons, and happy dancers fill the streets. Bands play while people clap and talk. What's going on? It's a Chinese New Year **celebration**!

5

# Different Dates

Chinese New Year is celebrated at the same time each year but not on the same dates. The holiday starts in January or February, when there is a new moon. It goes on for 15 days, until the full moon.

full moon

7

# How the Holiday Started

There is an old Chinese tale about a monster named Nian. As the new year began, Nian would start fights with people. The monster was afraid of loud noises and the color red. People wore red clothes and used fireworks to scare Nian away.

# Celebrating Around the World

People who live in China celebrate the Chinese New Year. Since Chinese people live all over the world, they celebrate where they are. In many cities in the United States, Chinese communities get together to celebrate. They have parades and dances.

**Chinese New Year parade,
New York City**

# Goodbye, Bad Luck

The Chinese New Year celebration has many **traditions**. One of them is cleaning before the New Year. People clean everything! Cleaning is a **symbol** for getting rid of bad luck. Good luck comes into the clean place.

## Family Time

Eating meals with the family is an important tradition. People often wear new red clothes. Some foods have special meanings. Round orange fruits mean happiness and riches. Rice cakes are a symbol for success. Tasty **dumplings** mean good luck.

Families and friends visit each other. They say, "Good luck" or, "Happiness for the family." Adults give children money in red **envelopes**. Guests bring oranges or other small gifts. In the Asian country of Singapore, guests give two oranges and get two oranges back.

## Lion and Dragon Dances

All during the celebration, there are lion and dragon dances. The lively dances take place in parades, parks, and meeting halls. The brave lion scares away the monster Nian. The dragon is a symbol of power and good luck.

## The Lantern Festival

It's the last night of the celebration. The full moon shines down on bright red **lanterns**. They hang in temples and homes and across streets. People carry them on walks. The lanterns mean joy and good luck for the new year!

# GLOSSARY

**celebration:** a time to show happiness for an event through activities such as eating or playing music

**dumpling:** a small piece of dough that may be filled with meat or vegetables and then cooked

**envelope:** a piece of paper that is folded to cover a card or letter

**lantern:** a lamp with a handle

**symbol:** a picture, shape, or object that stands for something else

**tradition:** having to do with long-practiced customs

# FOR MORE INFORMATION

## BOOKS

Compestine, Yin Chang. *D is for Dragon Dance*. New York: Holiday House, 2018.

Otto, Carolyn. *Holidays Around the World: Celebrate Chinese New Year: With Fireworks, Dragons, and Lanterns*. Washington, DC: National Geographic Children's Books, 2015.

## WEBSITES

**Chinese New Year Facts Kids Encyclopedia Facts**
*kids.kiddle.co/Chinese_New_Year*
Read about Chinese New Year celebrations and look at photographs of the celebration from China and around the world.

**Chinese New Year for Kids**
*www.china-family-adventure.com/chinese-new-year.html*
Learn all about Chinese New Year traditions, and get directions for making crafts.

# INDEX

cleaning  12

dance  10, 18

dragon  4, 18

food  14, 16

full moon  6, 20

luck  12, 14, 16, 18, 20

Nian  8, 18

parade  4, 10, 18

red  8, 14, 16, 20